Date: 3/15/12

J 796.323 WIS
Wiseman, Blaine.
Basketball /

THE GREATEST PLAYERS

BASKETBALL

Blaine Wiseman
and Aaron Carr

www.av2books.com

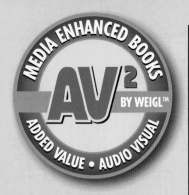

AV² provides enriched content that supplements and complements this book. Weigl's AV² books strive to create inspired learning and engage young minds in a total learning experience.

Your AV² Media Enhanced books come alive with...

Audio
Listen to sections of the book read aloud.

Key Words
Study vocabulary, and complete a matching word activity.

Video
Watch informative video clips.

Quizzes
Test your knowledge.

Embedded Weblinks
Gain additional information for research.

Slide Show
View images and captions, and prepare a presentation.

Try This!
Complete activities and hands-on experiments.

... and much, much more!

Go to **www.av2books.com**, and enter this book's unique code.

BOOK CODE

N498559

AV² by Weigl brings you media enhanced books that support active learning.

Published by AV² by Weigl
350 5ᵗʰ Avenue, 59ᵗʰ Floor
New York, NY 10118
Website: www.av2books.com   www.weigl.com

Library of Congress Cataloging-in-Publication Data

Wiseman, Blaine.
 Basketball / Blaine Wiseman and Aaron Carr.
   p. cm. -- (The greatest)
 Includes bibliographical references and index.
 ISBN 978-1-61690-698-6 (hardcover : alk. paper) -- ISBN 978-1-61690-703-7 (softcover : alk. paper)
 1. Basketball players--United States--Biography--Juvenile literature. I. Carr, Aaron. II. Title.
 GV884.A1W57 2012
 796.323092'2--dc22
 [B]
                              2011002300

Printed in the United States of America in North Mankato, Minnesota
2 3 4 5 6 7 8 9 0 15 14 13 12 11

102011
WEP211011

Project Coordinator Aaron Carr
Art Director Terry Paulhus

Photo Credits
Every reasonable effort has been made to trace ownership and to obtain permission to reprint copyright material. The publishers would be pleased to have any errors or omissions brought to their attention so that they may be corrected in subsequent printings.

Weigl acknowledges Getty Images as its primary image supplier for this title.

Contents

AV² Book Code 2

What is Basketball? 4

Michael Jordan 6

Magic Johnson 8

Larry Bird 10

Kobe Bryant.................... 12

LeBron James 14

Shaquille O'Neal 16

Cheryl Miller 18

Lisa Leslie 20

Wilt Chamberlain 22

Kareem Abdul-Jabbar 24

Greatest Moments 26

Write a Biography........... 28

Know Your Stuff! 30

Words to Know/Index 31

www.av2books.com 32

3

What is Basketball?

Introduction

The world of professional sports has a long history of great moments. The most memorable moments often come when the sport's greatest players overcome their most challenging obstacles. For the fans, these moments come to define their favorite sport. For the players, they stand as measuring posts of success.

Since the first National Basketball Association (NBA) game was played in 1946, fans of the sport have witnessed many great players and great moments. These moments include Michael Jordan's championship-winning shot in the last seconds of the game in 1999 and Wilt Chamberlain's 100-point game in 1962. Basketball has no shortage of these moments, when the sport's brightest stars accomplished feats that ensured they would be remembered as the greatest players.

Training Camp

Basketball is played by two teams that are each allowed five players on the court. The teams try to score points by shooting the ball through the hoop at the opposite end of the court. The team with the most points at the end of the game wins.

Basketball teams are usually organized into five main positions. These are center, point guard, shooting guard, power forward, and small forward. The players at each position play a unique role on the team. On offense, they try to move the ball to open players to score points. On defense, they try to keep the other team from scoring.

James Naismith invented basketball in 1891

The Basketball Court

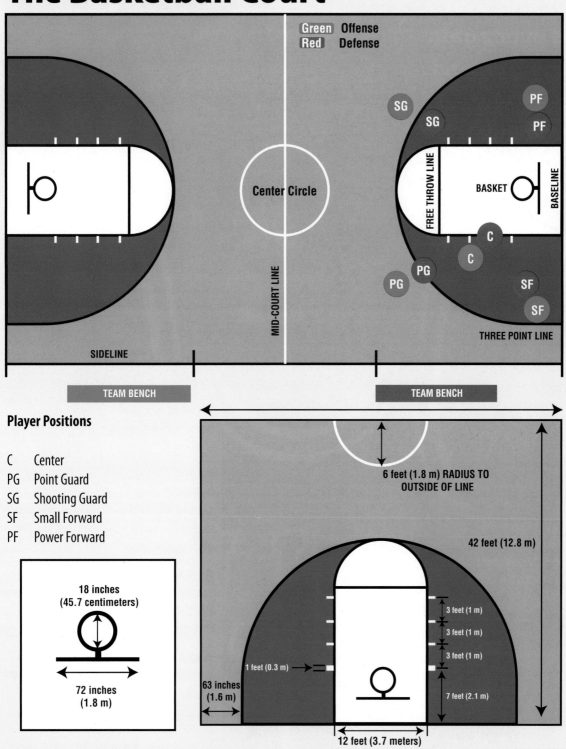

Green Offense
Red Defense

Center Circle

MID-COURT LINE

FREE THROW LINE

BASKET

BASELINE

THREE POINT LINE

SIDELINE

SG

SG

PF

PF

C

C

PG

PG

SF

SF

TEAM BENCH

TEAM BENCH

Player Positions

C   Center
PG   Point Guard
SG   Shooting Guard
SF   Small Forward
PF   Power Forward

18 inches
(45.7 centimeters)

72 inches
(1.8 m)

6 feet (1.8 m) RADIUS TO
OUTSIDE OF LINE

42 feet (12.8 m)

3 feet (1 m)
3 feet (1 m)
3 feet (1 m)

1 feet (0.3 m)

7 feet (2.1 m)

63 inches
(1.6 m)

12 feet (3.7 meters)

> "I've failed over and over and over again in my life, and that is why I succeed."

Michael Jordan

Jordan was known as "Air Jordan" for his spectacular jumping ability, which led to many memorable highlight-reel plays.

Player Profile

BORN Michael Jeffrey Jordan was born on February 17, 1963, in Brooklyn, New York.

FAMILY Jordan was the youngest of five children born to James and Deloris Jordan. He has two brothers and two sisters. Today, Jordan has two sons and one daughter.

EDUCATION Jordan graduated from E.A. Laney High School in Wilmington, North Carolina. He later attended the University of North Carolina.

AWARDS Six NBA championships, six NBA Finals **Most Valuable Player (MVP)** awards, five NBA MVP awards, three all-star game MVP awards, 1985 Rookie of the Year, 1988 Defensive Player of the Year, 14 all-star selections, 1984 and 1992 Olympic gold medal, named to NBA All-Time Team, inducted into the Basketball **Hall of Fame** in 2009

Michael Jordan
Shooting Guard

Early Years

As a child, Michael Jordan was a natural athlete. His favorite sport was baseball. He spent many hours developing his skills. In 1978, Jordan was cut from his high school basketball team. He trained and practiced all year.

Jordan's hard work earned the attention of the coach. Every time he felt tired, he would close his eyes and imagine the team roster without his name on it. This gave him the motivation to keep pushing himself to be the best he could be. Jordan made the team in his **junior** year. That season, he scored an average of 25 points per game.

Developing Skills

Jordan received a **scholarship** to play basketball for the University of North Carolina. In his first year, he had a great performance in the National Collegiate Athletic Association (NCAA) championship tournament. In the final game against Georgetown, Jordan scored the game-winning basket. The shot won the national championship for his team. Jordan was named College Player of the Year in each of his next two college seasons.

In 1984, Jordan was chosen to play for Team USA at the Olympics. He helped lead the team to a gold medal. In the **NBA draft**, Jordan was chosen by the Chicago Bulls with the third pick. Jordan became an instant star in the NBA, scoring 28.2 points per game, and winning the Rookie of the Year award. He would go on to become known as the greatest basketball player in history, winning six NBA championships. He was named finals MVP all six times. Jordan holds the record for highest career points per game average, with 30.1.

Michael Jordan

Greatest Moment

Jordan's greatest moments came while winning six NBA championships with the Chicago Bulls.

In 1998, the Bulls were playing the Utah Jazz in the Finals, trying to win their third championship in a row. Down by three points in the final seconds of game 6, Jordan drove the basket to bring his team within one point. Jordan then stole the ball from Karl Malone, and made the game-winning shot with only 5.2 seconds remaining, to give the Bulls their sixth NBA championship.

Michael Jordan dominated the NBA for his entire career, averaging 30.1 points per game in more than 1,000 games.

> "Ask not what your teammates can do for you. Ask what you can do for your teammates."
>
> Magic Johnson

At fix feet, nine inches tall, Magic Johnson was the tallest point guard in NBA history.

Player Profile

BORN Earvin Johnson, Jr. was born on August 14, 1959, in Lansing, Michigan.

FAMILY Johnson grew up in a large family. His parents, Earvin and Christine, had 10 children. Johnson is married and has three children.

EDUCATION He graduated from Everett High School, and later attended Michigan State University.

AWARDS Five NBA championships, three NBA Finals MVP awards, three NBA MVP awards, two all-star game MVP awards, 1992 Olympic gold medal, 12 all-star selections, named to NBA All-Time Team, inducted into the Basketball Hall of Fame in 2002

Earvin "Magic" Johnson
Point Guard

Early Years

As a child, Earvin Johnson lived to play basketball. He practiced his skills every chance he got. He even woke up early to spend time on the court before school. Johnson carried a basketball with him wherever he went. He would **dribble** with his right hand while he walked to the store, and with his left hand on the way back home.

Later, Johnson became a star basketball player at Everett High School. He led his team to the state championship with his incredible skill. His performance earned him a nickname that has stuck with him ever since, "Magic."

Developing Skills

Johnson's skills on the basketball court earned him a scholarship to Michigan State University. In his **freshman** year, he scored an average of 17 points per game and helped his team win the conference title. The following year, he was even more successful, as he led Michigan State to the NCAA championship game. They defeated Indiana State and their leader, Larry Bird, to win the national championship. This game began one of the greatest rivalries in sports, known as Magic versus Bird. Both stars would enter the NBA the following year and enjoy legendary careers, meeting in the NBA Finals three times.

Johnson holds the NBA all-time record for career assists per game average, with 11.2. His 10,141 assists are fourth all-time. In 13 NBA seasons, Johnson averaged 19.5 points per game.

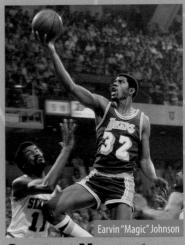
Earvin "Magic" Johnson

Greatest Moment

In his rookie season, Johnson and the Lakers advanced to the 1980 NBA Finals against the Philadelphia 76ers. In game 5, Lakers' star Kareem Abdul-Jabbar injured his ankle. He had scored 40 points that game, putting the Lakers within one win of the championship.

With Abdul-Jabbar unable to play in game 6, the 20-year-old Johnson had to lead the team. Johnson dominated the game, recording 42 points, 15 **rebounds**, seven **assists**, and three **steals**. The Lakers won the championship. It was one of the greatest rookie performances in sports history.

Johnson played his entire 13-year NBA career with the Los Angeles Lakers, leading them to five championships.

> "I've got a theory that if you give 100 percent all of the time, somehow things will work out in the end."
>
> Larry Bird

Larry Bird was known as one of the greatest team players of all time. It was his intelligence and ability to read the game that made him a superstar.

Player Profile

BORN Larry Joe Bird was born on December 7, 1956, in West Baden, Indiana.

FAMILY Bird was the fourth of six children born to Joe and Georgia Bird. He is married and has two daughters and a son.

EDUCATION Bird graduated from Springs Valley High School. He went on to graduate from Indiana State University with a degree in physical education.

AWARDS Three NBA championships, two NBA Finals MVP awards, three NBA MVP awards, 1980 Rookie of the Year, 1982 all-star game MVP, 1992 Olympic gold medal, 12 all-star selections, named to NBA All-Time Team, inducted into the Basketball Hall of Fame in 1998

Larry Bird
Forward

Early Years

Larry Bird grew up in the small town of French Lick, Indiana. His family was poor. Bird spent most of his time as a boy playing ball games with his brothers. Before they had a basketball hoop, the boys would try to throw a small sponge ball into a coffee can. Bird also played baseball and softball. He did not begin to focus on basketball until he started high school.

In his first two years of high school basketball, Bird did not stand out as a great player. In the summer of 1973, he grew four inches. Bird then started his **senior** year at 6 feet, 7 inches tall. His speed and agility, along with his height, made him a dominant player for his team. When he realized he had special abilities in basketball, Bird began practicing harder than ever before. He practiced all day and into the night. When he felt too tired, too sore, or too cold, he pushed himself to keep going. His work ethic combined with his size and ability made him popular with college scouts.

Developing Skills

Bird enrolled at Indiana State University. In his final season, he led his team to the NCAA championship game. Bird was named the 1978–1979 College Player of the Year. He graduated as the fifth highest scoring player in NCAA history.

Bird entered the NBA in the 1979–1980 season. He played all 13 seasons of his career with the Boston Celtics. He was named NBA MVP three years in a row from 1984 to 1986. Only two other players have ever won three straight MVPs. Bird scored 40 or more points in a game 47 times. In his career, Bird averaged 24 points, 10 rebounds, and 6 assists per game.

Larry Bird

Greatest Moment

In the 1987 playoffs, Bird and the Celtics were playing the Detroit Pistons. The Pistons had a 107–106 lead in game 5 with just seconds left on the clock. Detroit's Isaiah Thomas tried to make a pass to an open teammate. As the pass left his hands, Bird swooped in and stole the ball. He almost carried the ball out of bounds. However, Bird quickly regained his balance, turned toward the basket and made a pass to Dennis Johnson, who was breaking to the hoop. Johnson made the basket, and the Celtics won the game 108–107. They went on to win the series and advance to the NBA Finals.

After retiring, Larry Bird became the coach of the Indiana Pacers. In 1998, he was named NBA Coach of the Year. He is the only person to win MVP and Coach of the Year.

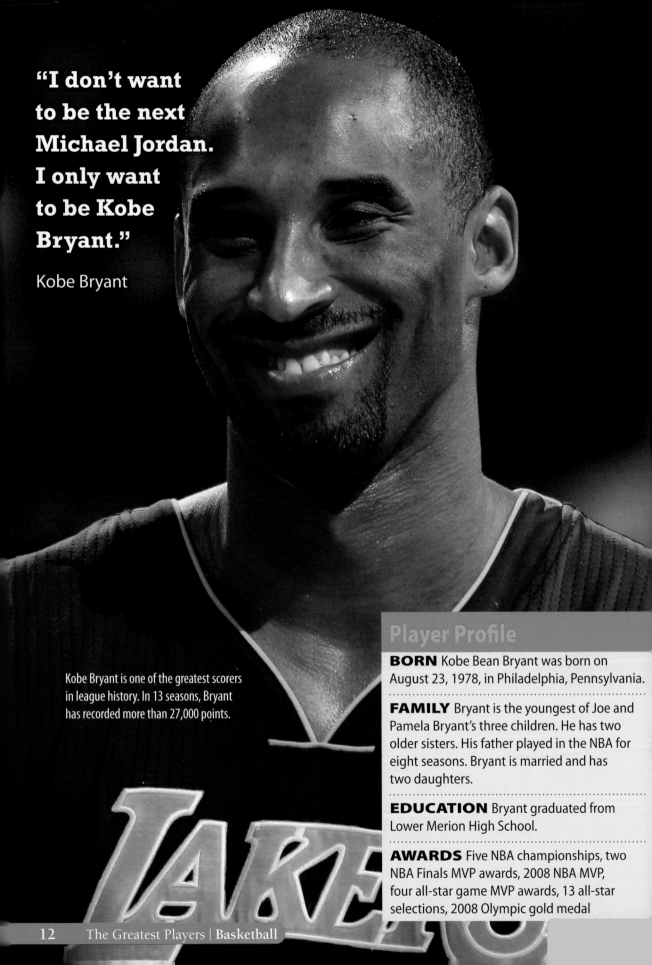

"I don't want to be the next Michael Jordan. I only want to be Kobe Bryant."

Kobe Bryant

Kobe Bryant is one of the greatest scorers in league history. In 13 seasons, Bryant has recorded more than 27,000 points.

Player Profile

BORN Kobe Bean Bryant was born on August 23, 1978, in Philadelphia, Pennsylvania.

FAMILY Bryant is the youngest of Joe and Pamela Bryant's three children. He has two older sisters. His father played in the NBA for eight seasons. Bryant is married and has two daughters.

EDUCATION Bryant graduated from Lower Merion High School.

AWARDS Five NBA championships, two NBA Finals MVP awards, 2008 NBA MVP, four all-star game MVP awards, 13 all-star selections, 2008 Olympic gold medal

Kobe Bryant
Shooting Guard

Early Years

Kobe Bryant was born in Philadelphia while his father, "Jellybean" Joe Bryant, was playing in the NBA for the Philadelphia 76ers. After his father's NBA career ended in 1984, the family moved to Italy, where his father continued playing professional basketball. Bryant practiced his basketball skills day and night, believing that he would one day play in the NBA. At age 13, Bryant's family returned to Philadelphia, where he began playing school basketball. By this time, Bryant knew he could be a star. He was even beating his dad in games of one-on-one.

Developing Skills

Having a basketball player for a father helped Bryant develop his skills. From an early age, he was surrounded by professional basketball players. They taught Bryant what it takes to be a great player. After his family moved back to Philadelphia, Bryant helped his high school team win the state championship. The team finished in last place the year before he joined. In 1995, Bryant's father arranged for his son to practice with members of the 76ers. Bryant once again had an opportunity to learn from professionals. He impressed the other players and coaches.

In 1996, Bryant became the youngest starter in NBA history when he joined the Los Angeles Lakers straight out of high school. Since then, he has become one of the greatest players in NBA history. Bryant led the Lakers to three straight NBA championships from 2000 to 2002. In more than 1,000 games played, he has averaged more than 25 points per game.

Kobe Bryant

Greatest Moment

Of Bryant's many great performances, his best came on January 22, 2006. During this game against the Toronto Raptors, he single-handedly led his team to a come-from-behind victory. In the process, he recorded one of the most impressive performances in NBA history.

Bryant sank 28 **field goals**, including seven **three-pointers**, and 18 **free throws** for an incredible 81 points. It was the second highest single game scoring effort in NBA history. Only Wilt Chamberlain has ever scored more points in one game.

Kobe Bryant has scored 50 points or more in a single game 24 times. This is the third most in NBA history behind only Wilt Chamberlain and Michael Jordan.

"Ask me to play. I'll play. Ask me to shoot. I'll shoot. Ask me to pass. I'll pass. Ask me to steal, block out, sacrifice, lead, dominate. Anything. But it's not what you ask of me. It's what I ask of myself."

LeBron James

LeBron James is often called "King James" for his dominating performances on the basketball court.

Player Profile

BORN LeBron Raymone James was born on December 30, 1984, in Akron, Ohio.

FAMILY James is the only child of Gloria James. He is married to Savannah Brinson. They have two sons, LeBron, Jr. and Bryce Maximus.

EDUCATION James graduated from St. Vincent-St. Mary's High School. He did not attend university.

AWARDS Two NBA MVP awards, two all-star game MVP awards, 2004 Rookie of the Year, seven all-star selections

LeBron James
Small Forward

Early Years

LeBron James was raised by his mother, Gloria. His father left Gloria to raise James by herself. She had trouble finding steady work. They lived in poor neighborhoods and had to move often. This lifestyle was challenging for James. He tried to relieve his frustration through sports. His favorite sports were basketball and football. When James started having problems in school, his coach, Frankie Walker, offered to help. He convinced Gloria to let James live with his family. With the help of the Walkers, James became an excellent student. Walker also helped James develop his basketball skills. James became friends and teammates with Walker's son, Frankie, Jr.

Developing Skills

In his first year of high school basketball, James led his team to a perfect record of 27 wins and no losses. When he was 17, James was invited to workout with the Cleveland Cavaliers. He impressed the coach by performing **slam dunks** over NBA players. After leading his team to a third high school state championship in four years, James decided to enter the NBA draft.

His hometown Ohio team, the Cleveland Cavaliers, had the first draft pick. They chose the 18-year-old James. Since then, James has become the most well known player in the NBA. After winning back-to-back league MVP awards, he moved to the Miami Heat in 2010. James is one of only two players ever to record 2,000 points, 500 rebounds, and 500 assists in a season five times. In 2011, James became the youngest player in NBA history to score 17,000 points.

LeBron James

Greatest Moment

James is one of the greatest players in the NBA. Unlike many great players, it did not take him long to get recognition.

In 2009, at only 24 years of age, James was named league MVP. This made him one of the youngest players in NBA history to win the award. That season, James led his team in points, assists, rebounds, blocked shots, and steals. The next year, he won his second straight MVP award. James is one of only 12 players in NBA history ever to win the award multiple times.

James is known for his incredible speed, skill, and strength, as well as his ability to read the game and see things on the court that others do not.

> "I did everything the right way and earned my spot in this game, nothing was given to me."
>
> Shaquille O'Neal

At 7 feet, 1 inch tall and 325 pounds, Shaquille O'Neal is one of the largest players to ever play in the NBA. His size earned him the nickname "Big Diesel."

Player Profile

BORN Shaquille Rashaun O'Neal was born on March 6, 1972, in Newark, New Jersey.

FAMILY O'Neal is the oldest of four children of mother Lucille O'Neal and step-father Phil Harrison. He has two sisters and a brother. O'Neal has five children.

EDUCATION O'Neal graduated from Cole High School. He later graduated from Louisiana State University with a bachelor of arts degree. He earned a master's degree in business from the University of Phoenix.

AWARDS Four NBA championships, three NBA Finals MVP awards, 2000 NBA league MVP, 1996 Olympic gold medal, 1993 Rookie of the Year, three all-star game MVP awards, 15 all-star selections

Shaquille O'Neal
Center

Early Years

Shaquille O'Neal spent his early years in the tough parts of Newark and Jersey City. His step-father was a U.S. Army sergeant. Spending his teenage years on an army base gave O'Neal the discipline he needed to become successful. By age 13, O'Neal was 6 feet, 6 inches tall. He was a force on the basketball court, but he also had a temper. He got into fights with other kids and was nearly thrown out of school. With help from his step-father, O'Neal became an excellent student who got along with other kids.

At age 15, O'Neal's family moved to San Antonio, Texas. There, he attended Cole High School. Though the team was winning, O'Neal's father did not like his son's effort. His father told him that if he was not going to try his best, he should quit. This inspired O'Neal to be better.

Developing Skills

In 1990, O'Neal joined the Louisiana State University team. In his second season, he became the first player to ever lead his conference in scoring, rebounding, field goal percentage, and blocked shots. Although he was already good, his coach knew that O'Neal still needed help to become great. He asked NBA legends Bill Walton and Kareem Abdul-Jabbar to tutor O'Neal.

O'Neal was drafted by the Orlando Magic in 1992. He is one of only three players ever to win the league MVP, Finals MVP, and the all-star game MVP in the same season. O'Neal ranks fifth in all-time scoring with 28,590 points.

Shaquille O'Neal

Greatest Moment

In the 2001 NBA Finals, the Los Angeles Lakers were competing for their second straight league championship. After losing game 1 to the Philadelphia 76ers, O'Neal was determined to take back momentum for the Lakers. In one of the greatest individual playoff performances of all-time, "Big Diesel" recorded 28 points, 20 rebounds, nine assists, and a record-tying eight blocks. The Lakers won the game 98–89 to even the series. With momentum on their side, the Lakers went on to win the next three games to win the series. O'Neal won his second straight NBA Finals MVP award.

Shaquille O'Neal was only the second player in NBA history to win three NBA Finals MVP awards in a row. Michael Jordan is the only other player to do this.

> **"I was just someone who loved the game so very much and had a passion for sport and life."**
>
> Cheryl Miller

Many people consider Cheryl Miller to be the greatest female basketball player of all time.

Player Profile

BORN Cheryl Miller was born on January 3, 1964, in Riverside, California.

FAMILY Miller is one of five children born to parents Saul and Carrie Miller. She has a sister and three brothers. Her brother, Reggie, played in the NBA, and her brother, Darrell, played Major League Baseball.

EDUCATION Miller graduated from Riverside Polytechnic High School. She later graduated from the University of Southern California with a degree in Communications.

AWARDS NCAA Finals MVP in 1983 and 1984, three Naismith Awards as the best U.S. female college basketball player, 1985 Wade Trophy winner as the top female player in the NCAA, inducted into the Basketball Hall of Fame in 1995

Cheryl Miller
Forward

Early Years

Cheryl Miller was born into a talented family. The Millers demanded a strong work ethic from their children. As a child, Miller's passion was basketball. Competing against her older, bigger brothers on the family's backyard court made Miller a strong player. As she grew and became more skilled, her younger brother, Reggie, challenged neighborhood boys to play games against him and his sister. The boys accepted, expecting an easy win. Miller dominated the games, however, and earned the respect of everyone she played. Miller's size gave her an advantage in basketball. In high school, she was 6 feet, 2 inches tall.

Developing Skills

In 1978, Miller joined her high school basketball team and became an instant success. She dominated the league, scoring 3,405 points over four years. She scored an average of 37 points per game. In one game, she set a California high school record with 105 points. In her four years of high school, Miller led her team to four straight state championships. Her team won 132 games and only lost four. She also became known as the first woman to perform a slam dunk in an organized game.

Heading into college, Miller was the most **recruited** female athlete of all time. She was offered scholarships to more than 250 colleges and universities. Miller chose the University of Southern California. There, she led the team to two straight NCAA Championships. Miller was named MVP both years. Throughout her college career, she averaged 23 points and 11.9 rebounds per game.

Cheryl Miller

Greatest Moment

After college, Miller was one of the most popular athletes in the United States. She was also one of the most famous basketball players in the world.

In the 1984 Summer Olympics in Los Angeles, Miller led Team USA to its first ever gold medal in women's basketball. The team won each of its six games by no less than 28 points. Miller was the top player in the Olympics. In the gold medal game, she led the way with 16 points, 11 rebounds, and five assists. With Miller leading the way, Team USA defeated South Korea 85–55.

Cheryl Miller used her degree in communications and her experience in basketball to launch a career as a sports reporter and commentator.

"It's about work ethic. Winning never gets old."

Lisa Leslie

Lisa Leslie has helped lead Team USA to four Olympic gold medals in women's basketball.

Player Profile

BORN Lisa Deshaun Leslie was born on July 7, 1972, in Los Angeles, California.

FAMILY Leslie was born to parents Christine and Walter Leslie. She has two sisters. Leslie is married with two children.

EDUCATION Leslie graduated from Morningside High School. She later graduated from the University of Southern California with a degree in communications. Leslie earned a master's degree in business administration from the University of Phoenix.

AWARDS Two Women's National Basketball Association (WNBA) championships, two WNBA Finals MVP awards, three WNBA league MVP awards, four Olympic gold medals, two Defensive Player of the Year awards, three all-star game MVP awards, eight all-star selections

Lisa Leslie
Center

Early Years

As the tallest girl at her school, Lisa Leslie was often teased by her classmates. Her mother, who was 6 feet, 3 inches tall, told her to be proud of her height and that she was beautiful. This advice helped Leslie use her height to her advantage. Although she was not interested in basketball, her middle school classmates begged her to join their team because she was so tall. Leslie joined the team and led them to an undefeated season in her first year.

In her second year of high school, Leslie and her family moved to a different part of the city. At her new high school, Leslie became a basketball star. She once scored 101 points in the first half alone. The game ended at halftime because the other team **forfeited**. Leslie was only five points away from breaking Cheryl Miller's record for most points scored in one game.

Developing Skills

With such great success in high school, Leslie chose to play college basketball for the University of Southern California. During her college career, she was named Freshman of the Year and National College Player of the Year. When the WNBA started in 1997, the Los Angeles Sparks drafted Leslie.

In 12 seasons with the Sparks, Leslie scored 6,263 points. Only one other WNBA player has scored more than 6,000 career points. She also leads the league in all-time career rebounds, with 3,307. Her 822 blocked shots is second on the all-time list. In 2008, Leslie became the first team sport athlete to win four straight Olympic gold medals.

Lisa Leslie

Greatest Moment

After college, Leslie's dream was to play in the Olympics. She got her chance in the 1996 Summer Olympics in Atlanta, Georgia.

The team trained for a year before the tournament began. Knowing that she was an important part of the team, Leslie worked harder than ever to prepare. Team USA won all eight of its games in the tournament. In the gold medal game, Team USA defeated the 1994 World Champions, Brazil. Leslie was the star of the tournament. She capped it off with 29 points in the final game. She has since won three more Olympic gold medals.

Lisa Leslie was the first woman to ever perform a slam dunk in the WNBA.

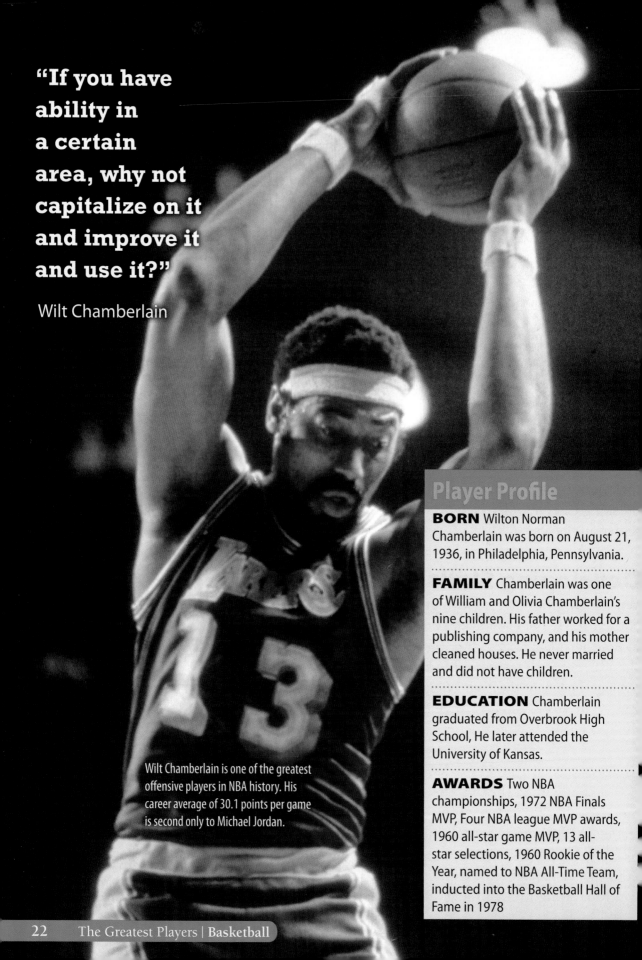

"If you have ability in a certain area, why not capitalize on it and improve it and use it?"

Wilt Chamberlain

Wilt Chamberlain is one of the greatest offensive players in NBA history. His career average of 30.1 points per game is second only to Michael Jordan.

Player Profile

BORN Wilton Norman Chamberlain was born on August 21, 1936, in Philadelphia, Pennsylvania.

FAMILY Chamberlain was one of William and Olivia Chamberlain's nine children. His father worked for a publishing company, and his mother cleaned houses. He never married and did not have children.

EDUCATION Chamberlain graduated from Overbrook High School, He later attended the University of Kansas.

AWARDS Two NBA championships, 1972 NBA Finals MVP, Four NBA league MVP awards, 1960 all-star game MVP, 13 all-star selections, 1960 Rookie of the Year, named to NBA All-Time Team, inducted into the Basketball Hall of Fame in 1978

Wilt Chamberlain
Center

Early Years

At 7 feet, 1 inch tall and 275 pounds, Wilt Chamberlain was known by nicknames like Wilt "The Stilt" and "The Big Dipper." Chamberlain was always tall and athletic. By the time he was 10 years old, he was already 6 feet tall. Chamberlain began playing basketball in junior high school and quickly fell in love with the game. His size, speed, and jumping ability made him an instant success in basketball. By the time Chamberlain reached high school, he was unstoppable on the basketball court.

Chamberlain was much more than just the tallest, fastest, and strongest player on the court. He also had the ability to see the game differently than other players. In three years of high school basketball, Chamberlain scored 2,252 points.

Developing Skills

Chamberlain only played two years of college basketball for the University of Kansas. In that time, he was so dominant on the court that several rules had to be changed to make the game fair for other players. Rather than returning to university for another season, Chamberlain decided to become a professional basketball player.

At that time, the NBA only accepted college players who completed their studies. This forced Chamberlain to wait one year before he could join the NBA. Instead, he joined the **Harlem Globetrotters**. In 1959, he entered the NBA with his hometown Philadelphia Warriors. That season, he became the first player in NBA history to win both Rookie of the Year and MVP honors.

Wilt Chamberlain

Greatest Moment

In the 1961–62 season, Chamberlain became a part of NBA history. Scoring 50 points in a single game is a benchmark for the great players in basketball. That season, Chamberlain averaged 50.4 points per game. On March 2, 1962, Chamberlain recorded one of the greatest individual performances in the history of the NBA. That game, he scored 100 points against the New York Knicks. Chamberlain's average of 50.4 points per game that season is an NBA record that still stands. He also scored 4,029 points that year. This is the most points ever scored in a single NBA season.

Wilt Chamberlain is tied with Michael Jordan for the NBA record for most consecutive seasons leading the league in scoring. Both players did this seven times.

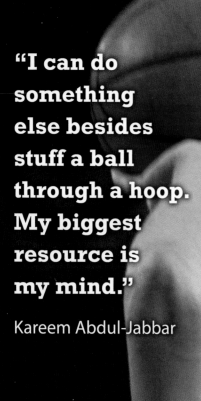

"I can do something else besides stuff a ball through a hoop. My biggest resource is my mind."

Kareem Abdul-Jabbar

Kareem Abdul-Jabbar holds all-time NBA records for most career points, most field goals made, and most all-star selections.

Player Profile

BORN Ferdinand Lewis Alcindor, Jr. was born on April 16, 1947, in New York, New York.

FAMILY Abdul-Jabbar is an only child. He was raised by parents Ferdinand and Lillian in New York City. He has two daughters and three sons.

EDUCATION Abdul-Jabbar graduated from Power Memorial Academy. He later graduated from the University of California, Los Angeles (UCLA).

AWARDS Six NBA championships, two NBA Finals MVP awards, six NBA league MVP awards, 1970 Rookie of the Year, 19 all-star selections, named to the NBA All-Time Team, inducted into the Basketball Hall of Fame in 1995

Kareem Abdul-Jabbar

Center

Early Years

Kareem Abdul-Jabbar was named after his father, Ferdinand Lewis Alcindor, but he was usually called Lew. In his teens, he began growing very quickly. He started playing basketball and soon became known for his skills on the court. Lew also worked hard in school. He wanted to play in the NBA, but his parents made sure he stayed focused on school as well.

In high school, Lew was already 6 feet, 8 inches tall. He made the varsity team in his freshman year. The next season, he averaged 19 points per game and led his team to a city championship. Lew continued to improve, and won two more city championships. He averaged 33 points per game in his final high school season.

Developing Skills

After high school, Lew moved to Los Angeles to attend UCLA. In his first game, he scored 56 points. By the end of his college career, Lew had led the Bruins to three straight NCAA championships. He won the MVP award all three years. Years later, he was voted the greatest college basketball player in history.

After college, Lew joined the NBA. He converted to Islam and changed his name to Kareem Abdul-Jabbar. This means "noble, powerful servant." Under his new name, he had one of the most dominant careers in NBA history. Abdul-Jabbar retired holding many records, including most career points, with 38,387, and most league MVP awards, with six.

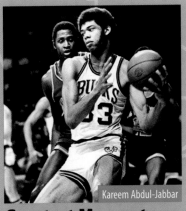
Kareem Abdul-Jabbar

Greatest Moment

On April 5, 1984, Abdul-Jabbar became the greatest scorer in NBA history. That night, he broke Wilt Chamberlain's points record. Only one point behind Chamberlain, Abdul-Jabbar took a pass from his young teammate, Magic Johnson. The only person standing in his way was Mark Eaton of the Utah Jazz, one of the tallest players in NBA history at 7 feet, 4 inches tall. Abdul-Jabbar faked to his right, then spun to his left and unleashed his famous "sky hook" shot, arcing the ball high in the air and through the hoop. It was his 31,240th career point.

Kareem Abdul-Jabbar's record of 38,387 career points is almost 2,000 points more than his closest competitor and about 10,000 more than any current player.

Greatest Moments

1970 – Inspiring Reed

When: May 8, 1970

Where: New York, New York

The New York Knicks were one win away from the NBA championship when team captain Willis Reed tore a leg muscle. The Lakers won the next game to even the series. Then, seconds before the start of game 7, Reed walked onto the court. He scored the first two baskets for the Knicks. Reed only scored four points, but he inspired his teammates. The Knicks won 113-99. It was their first championship.

1980
Magic Johnson scores 42 points, 15 rebounds, and seven assists in game 6 of the NBA finals.

1984
Cheryl Miller leads Team US to its first eve gold medal in women's Olymp basketball.

1960   1970   1980   1985   1990

1962
Wilt Chamberlain scores 100 points in a single game.

1976 – Basketball's Greatest Game

When: June 4, 1976

Where: Boston, Massachusetts

In game 5 of the NBA championship, the Boston Celtics and the Phoenix Suns went into double overtime. With four seconds left, John Havlicek hit a running shot to give the Celtics the lead. Refusing to admit defeat, Gar Heard of the Suns took one last shot before the buzzer. The shot was good, and the teams headed into triple overtime. The Celtics rallied in the third overtime and won the game 128-126.

1984
Kareem Abdul-Jabbar takes over the all-time NBA points lead.

1986
Larry Bird wins his third straight league MVP award.

1987 – Captain Hook

When: June 9, 1987

Where: Boston, Massachusetts

The Lakers were holding a one-point lead late in game 4 of their playoff series against the Boston Celtics. With just 12 seconds on the clock, Larry Bird sank a three-pointer to put the Celtics up by two points. With time running out, Magic Johnson took a running hook shot over a swarm of defenders. The shot went in with only two seconds left. The Lakers won the game and went on to win the championship.

2006
Kobe Bryant nets 81 points in a game versus the Toronto Raptors.

2011
LeBron James becomes the youngest player ever to score 17,000 career points.

1995	2000	2005	2010	2015

1996
Lisa Leslie leads Team USA to an Olympic gold medal.

1998 – Mr. Clutch Performance

When: June 14, 1998

Where: Salt Lake City, Utah

In game 6 of the NBA championship, the Chicago Bulls were 41 seconds away from going back to Utah for game 7. Then, Michael Jordan stepped up with one of the greatest clutch performances in NBA history. He hit a **lay-up** to bring the Bulls to within one point of tying the game. Then, Jordan stole the ball from Karl Malone and broke for the net. He sank a last-second jump shot to win the his sixth championship in eight years.

2001
Shaquille O'Neal records 28 points, 20 rebounds, nine assists, and eight blocks in game 2 of the NBA Finals.

Write a Biography

Life Story

A person's life story can be the subject of a book. This kind of book is called a biography. Biographies often describe the lives of people who have achieved great success. These people may be alive today, or they may have lived many years ago. Reading a biography can help you learn more about a great person.

Get the Facts

Use this book, and research in the library and on the Internet, to find out more about your favorite basketball player. Learn as much about this player as you can. What team did this person play for? What are his or her statistics in important categories? Has this person set any records? Be sure to also write down key events in the person's life. What was this person's childhood like? What has he or she accomplished? Is there anything else that makes this person special or unusual?

Use the Concept Web

A concept web is a useful research tool. Read the questions in the concept web on the following page. Answer the questions in your notebook. Your answers will help you write a biography.

- What did you learn from the books you read in your research?
- Would you suggest these books to others?
- Was anything missing from these books?

- Where does this individual currently reside?
- Does he or she have a family?

- Where and when was this person born?
- Describe his or her parents, siblings, and friends.
- Did this person grow up in unusual circumstances?

Your Opinion

Adulthood

Childhood

WRITING A BIOGRAPHY

Main Accomplishments

Help and Obstacles

Work and Preparation

- What is this person's life's work?
- Has he or she received awards or recognition for accomplishments?
- How have this person's accomplishments served others?

- Did this individual have a positive attitude?
- Did he or she receive help from others?
- Did this person have a mentor?
- Did this person face any hardships?
- If so, how were the hardships overcome?

- What was this person's education?
- What was his or her work experience?
- How does this person work; what is the process he or she uses?

Know your STUFF!

1 Who set the NBA record for most points in a game by one player?

2 What feat has only been accomplished by Michael Jordan and Shaquille O'Neal?

3 Who is the all-time point scoring leader in the NBA?

4 Who led the United States to its first ever women's basketball Olympic gold medal?

5 Who holds the NBA record for highest career points per game average? What is the average?

6 When Kareem Abdul-Jabbar was injured in game 6 of the 1980 NBA final, who was the rookie that stepped in to take his place?

7 In 2011, LeBron James became the youngest player ever to do what?

8 Kobe Bryant recorded the second highest single-game point total with how many points?

9 Who is the only team sport athlete to win four straight Olympic gold medals?

10 What did Larry Bird accomplish that only two other players have ever done?

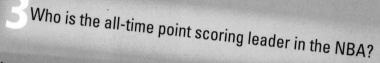

ANSWERS: 1. Wilt Chamberlain with 100 points 2. Winning three NBA Finals MVP awards in a row 3. Kareem Abdul-Jabbar 4. Cheryl Miller 5. Michael Jordan at 30.1 points per game 6. Magic Johnson 7. Score 17,000 career points 8. 81 9. Lisa Leslie 10. Win three straight league MVP awards

Glossary

ssists: a pass that leads directly to a field goal

ribble: bouncing the ball off the floor; allows the player to move around the court with the ball

eld goals: a shot that results in the ball going through the net from above; scores two points

orfeited: quit the game, losing automatically

ree throw: a free shot at the net awarded by a referee; scores one point

reshman: first year

all of Fame: a place in Springfield, Massachusetts, honoring the greatest players in basketball history

arlem Globetrotters: a traveling basketball team that combines elements of theatre and comedy into their games

unior: third year

ay-up: a one-handed shot from close to the basket, usually by bouncing the ball off the backboard

Most Valuable Player (MVP): a person judged to be the most valuable to his or her team's success

NBA draft: a process of selecting young players to join the NBA

rebounds: when a player grabs the ball after it comes off the net or backboard after a failed field goal attempt

recruited: trying to convince someone to join

rivalries: ongoing competitions for the same goal

roster: the list of people on a team

scholarship: money awarded to support a student's education

senior: fourth and final year

slam dunks: shots in which the player jumps and slams the ball through the net

starter: players chosen to start the game for their team

steals: when a defending player takes the ball from his or her opponent

three-pointers: a field goal from behind the three-point line; scores three points

Index

bdul-Jabbar, Kareem 9, 17, 24, 25, 26, 30

ird, Larry 9, 10, 11, 26, 27, 30
ryant, Kobe 12, 13, 27, 30

enter 4, 5, 17, 21, 23, 25
hamberlain, Wilt 4, 13, 22, 23, 25, 26, 30

orward 4, 5, 11, 15, 19

uard 4, 5, 7, 8, 9, 13

all of Fame 6, 8, 10, 18, 22, 24

mes, LeBron 14, 15, 27, 30
hnson, Earvin "Magic" 8, 9, 25, 26, 27, 30

Jordan, Michael 4, 6, 7, 12, 13, 17, 22, 23, 27, 30

Leslie, Lisa 20, 21, 27, 30

Miller, Cheryl 18, 19, 21, 26, 30
Most Valuable Player (MVP) 6, 7, 8, 10, 11, 12, 14, 15, 16, 17, 18, 19, 20, 22, 23, 24, 25, 26, 30

National Basketball Association (NBA) 4, 6, 7, 8, 9, 10, 11, 12, 13, 14, 15, 16, 17, 18, 22, 23, 24, 25, 26, 27, 30
National Collegiate Athletic Association (NCAA) 7, 9, 11, 18, 19, 25

O'Neal, Shaquille 16, 17, 27, 30

slam dunk 15, 19, 21

Women's National Basketball Association (WNBA) 20, 21

Log on to www.av2books.com

AV² by Weigl brings you media enhanced books that support active learning. Go to www.av2books.com, and enter the special code found on page 2 of this book. You will gain access to enriched and enhanced content that supplements and complements this book. Content includes video, audio, web links, quizzes, a slide show, and activities.

Audio
Listen to sections of the book read aloud.

Video
Watch informative video clips.

Embedded Weblinks
Gain additional information for research.

Try This!
Complete activities and hands-on experiments.

WHAT'S ONLINE?

Try This!	Embedded Weblinks	Video	EXTRA FEATURES
Try a basketball activity. Test your knowledge of basketball equipment. Complete a mapping activity.	Learn more about basketball players. Read about basketball coaches. Find out more about where basketball games take place.	Watch a video about basketball. View stars of the sport in action. Watch a video about basketball players.	**Audio** Listen to sections of the book read aloud. **Key Words** Study vocabulary, and complete a matching word activity. **Slide Show** View images and captio and prepare a presentat **Quizzes** Test your knowledge.

AV² was built to bridge the gap between print and digital. We encourage you to tell us what you like and what you want to see in the future.

Sign up to be an AV² Ambassador at www.av2books.com/ambassador.